A Company of Actors

PUBLICATIONS
of the
Dramatic Museum
OF COLUMBIA UNIVERSITY
IN THE CITY OF NEW YORK

Fifth Series

Papers on Acting

I 'THE ART OF ACTING,' by Dion Boucicault, with an introduction by Otis Skinner.

II 'ACTORS AND ACTING,' a discussion by Constant Coquelin, Henry Irving, and Dion Boucicault.

III 'ON THE STAGE,' by Frances Anne Kemble, with an introduction by George Arliss.

IV 'A COMPANY OF ACTORS,' by Francisque Sarcey, with an introduction by Brander Matthews.

PAPERS ON ACTING

IV

A Company of Actors

(The Comédie Française)

BY

FRANCISQUE SARCEY

WITH AN INTRODUCTION BY
BRANDER MATTHEWS

Published for the
Dramatic Museum of Columbia University
in the City of New York

Columbia University Press
MCMXXVI

CONTENTS

In 1871, during the dark days of the commune in Paris, a number of the members of the Comédie-Française headed by Got went over to London for a brief season, earning money which helped to support the company of the House of Molière; and in the spring and early summer of 1879 the entire company paid a visit to London while the Théâtre Français was being repaired and redecorated. The season lasted for six weeks and at every performance the Gaiety Theater had to turn away many playgoers who wanted to profit by the opportunity to study the foremost company in Europe, then at the moment of its most brilliant prosperity.

The French organization was accompanied to England by Francisque Sarcey, the most important French dramatic critic of his time. He was as expert in expounding the principles and the practices of the art of acting as he was in declaring those of the art of playmaking; and he was as familiar with the annals of the French theater as he was with the history of the French drama. He had earlier published ' Comédiens et Comédiennes,' a series of biographical and critical studies of the leading members of the Comédie-Française; and no one else was as well equipt as he to explain the organization of the Comédie-Française, to describe its traditions, and to expound the unwritten laws which assure its stability. This he did in a lecture delivered one afternoon at the Gaiety Theater, on the stage of which the Comédie-Française was appearing every evening. At the request of James Knowles, the editor of the *Nineteenth Century*, he wrote out his lecture, which was translated into English by M. Barbier and published in that monthly review in the number for July, 1879.

Henry James, an assiduous attendant at the Théâtre Français, whenever he was in Paris had taken Sarcey's ' Comédiens et Comédiennes ' as the text for an essay on the Théâtre Français, originally published in the *Galaxy* and later reprinted in his volume on ' French Poets and Novelists ' (1878). He

dwelt with reminiscent delight on the satis-
faction he had always had in taking his seat
in that noble theater and he emphasized the
main point that Sarcey brought out clearly: —

The traditions of the Comédie-Française — that
is the sovereign word, and that is the charm of
the place — the charm that one never ceases to
feel, however often one may sit beneath the classic,
dusky dome. One feels this charm with peculiar
intensity as a newly arrived foreigner. The
Théâtre Française has had the good fortune to
be able to allow its traditions to accumulate. They
have been preserved, transmitted, respected, cher-
ished, until at last they form the very atmosphere,
the vital air, of the establishment. A stranger
feels their superior influence the first time he sees
the great curtain go up; he feels that he is in a
theater that is not as other theaters are. It is not
only better, it is different. It has a peculiar perfection — something consecrated, historical, aca-
demic. This impression is delicious, and he
watches the performance in a sort of tranquil
ecstasy.

It may be noted here that Henry James
was not as careful as he might be to observe
the distinction Sarcey scrupulously makes between the Comédie-Française, which is the
organization itself, the company of come-
dians and tragedians, and the Théâtre Fran-

çais, which is the name of the building that happens now to be the home of the organization — the august company in its two centuries and a half of existence having migrated half a dozen times from one worthy edifice to another.

After the Comédie-Française had brought to an end its triumphant season in England, Matthew Arnold wrote a pungent paper on the 'French Play in London' (republished in his 'Irish Essays' [1882]). He was an old playgoer, missing no opportunity to see the best that could be afforded by the playhouses of England, France and Germany. In the course of his essay he recorded his intense admiration for Rachel — whose exquisite art he had commemorated in three sonnets — he contrasted the dramatic poetry of the French with that of the English, to the advantage of the latter; and he expressed his dissatisfaction with the later social drama popular in his time in Paris, the plays of Augier and the younger Dumas. But he was cordial in his praise of the French players and of the organization which gave them occasion to display their histrionic gifts to the best advantage. And he seized the chance to point a moral for the benefit of his fellow-countrymen: —

What then, finally, *are* we to learn from the marvellous success and attractiveness of the performances at the Gaiety Theater? What *is* the consequence which is right and rational for us to draw? Surely it is this: "The theater is irresistible; *organize the theater.*" Surely, if we wish to stand less in our own way, and to have clever notions of the consequences of things, it is to this conclusion we must come.

The performances of the French company show plainly, I think, what is gained, — the theater being admitted to be an irresistible need for civilized communities, — by organizing the theater. Some of the drama played by this company is, as we have seen, questionable. But, in the absence of an organization such as this, it would be played even yet more; it would, with a still lower drama to accompany it, almost if not altogether reign; it would have far less correction and relief by better things. An older and better drama containing many things of high merit, some things of surpassing merit, is kept before the public by means of this company, is given to perfection. Pieces of truth and beauty, which emerge here and there among the questionable pieces of the modern drama, get the benefit of this company's skill, and are given to perfection. The questionable pieces themselves lose something of their unprofitableness and vice in their hands; the acting carries us into

5

the world of correct and pleasing art, if the piece does not. And the type of perfection fixt by these fine actors influences for good every actor in France.

Moreover, the French company shows us not only what is gained by organizing the theater, but what is meant by organizing it. The organization in the example before us is simple and rational.

To *Munsey's Magazine* for September, 1908 I contributed an account of the vicissitudes of the Comédie-Française in which I asserted that any attempt to duplicate the French institution in Great Britain or the United States would be difficult, not to say impossible: —

To suggest an English equivalent for this French institution we should have to imagine that the performers of the York or the Coventry plays had established themselves in London, and that their rude playhouse had been taken over by Shakspere and his comrades. We should have to imagine further that this company, having acted the chief plays of the Elizabethan dramatists, survived the Commonwealth and was transferred under the Restoration to Drury Lane, where it performed the comedies of Congreve and Wycherly, Vanbrugh, and Farquhar. We must imagine, also, that this company, to which Burbage and Betterton had belonged, welcomed in time Garrick and Cooke, the Kembles and the Keans, Macready and Irving; and that after producing the comedies of Sheridan and Goldsmith, it had been hospitable in time to the later plays of Gilbert and Pinero, Henry Arthur Jones and James M. Barrie, preserving unbroken the splendid traditions bequeathed to it by the past.

And yet, even if a rival to the Comédie-Française cannot now be achieved in London or in New York, it might at least be attempted. Even if there is not now in any theater of the English-speaking world the historic continuity which has given stability and longevity to the Comédie-Française, we have the material for the organization for which Matthew Arnold pleaded; we have in Great Britain and the United States actors and actresses unsurpassed in France, and we have dramatists no longer inferior. Even if traditions cannot be improvised, we might begin to create men now for the benefit of those who are coming after us, in the hope that one or another may take root to burgeon abundantly in the future.

Here in New York we have a model; we have here an organization for the opera, which has endured now for more than a generation and which shows few signs of lessening vitality. We may very well ask ourselves if the devotion and the generosity which has done so much for the prosperity of the music-drama might not be enlisted for the support of the drama. To create an institution which may in the years to come, withstand comparison with the Comédie-Française will take time and wisdom and money; it will demand not a little of each of these elements of permanence, but the result would be worth while.

BRANDER MATTHEWS

A COMPANY OF ACTORS

,

THE COMÉDIE-FRANÇAISE

I

Ladies and Gentlemen, — In addressing a public before whom I have the honor to appear for the first time, I ought to speak of the emotion I feel, and, at the same time, solicit your indulgence. Such is the usual exordium of lecturers when making their début. But the truth is, I am not moved in any way, and do not feel the shadow of a fear. It is your fault if I express this unwonted confidence, and you have only yourselves to thank for it. The fact is that, ever since I landed on the hospitable shores of England, I have met with so much courtesy, kindness, and attention — a cordiality so frank and so obliging — that, in speaking to you, I feel as if I were addressing my friends at home rather than my hosts abroad. Hence

I do not think it necessary to solicit an indulgence which I feel sure you have already granted to me.

I am about to speak to you of the Comédie-Française and its organisation, and particularly the latter point, for it is the organisation of that institution which constitutes its power and greatness. It is, in fact, owing to that organisation that it is able to-day to lay before your eyes the imposing and marvellous sight it offers to the world.

The Comédie-Française took possession of the Gaiety Theatre a few weeks ago, and during this lapse of time a fresh bill has been issued every day, and every night a series of new plays submitted to your judgment. This ever-changing variety will continue to the end of its stay in London. The Comédie-Française intends to remain here for forty-five days, and its programme comprises forty-three plays. These forty-three pieces constitute only a small portion of its repertory. Thus, although four or five of the dramatic masterpieces of Corneille are constantly played in Paris, only one, the ' Menteur,' a comedy, has been selected for representation here; Racine also is represented by only one tragedy; from Molière three or four comedies have been chosen, while Regnard and Beaumarchais supply but one work each — the 'Joueur' and the 'Barbier de Séville.' The names of Lesage and Marivaux are altogether absent. Coming lower down, Scribe, who contributed so much to the Comédie-Française, is likewise absent; and as to contemporary dramatic authors, we shall see with regret what an amount of dramatic treasure the Comédie-Française has been obliged to leave aside.

The *répertoire courant* — that is to say, the pieces which the company can play at any moment, all the parts being known beforehand, without any other preparation than one of those summary rehearsals known in the language of the French green-room as *raccords* — its *répertoire courant* includes about one hundred plays, out of which the manager can choose as he likes. A single order to the storekeeper, a notice posted up in the green-room, is all that is required: the same night the scenery is ready, all appurtenances in order, and the actors at their posts.

Need I tell you that all the plays are acted with remarkable *ensemble?* You have been

able during the past fortnight to ascertain this
fact by your own experience; and I find by
your papers that it is precisely the perfection
of that *ensemble* which has most deeply
struck the theatrical critics of the English
press.   At the Comédie-Française the most
insignificant parts are filled up, if not by first-
class actors, at least by persons who have already studied long and know their business.
In plays like 'Hernani' and 'Mademoi-
selle de Belle-Isle,' for instance, in which, as
you may have seen, there are a certain number of very secondary personages, some of
whom have but a few words to utter, while
others say nothing at all, these obscure parts,
instead of being given up to common super-
numeraries engaged for the night, are filled
either by young actors who have their trial
to go through, or by old actors who have no
other talent but their perfect knowledge of
the boards — in short, by actors who form
part of the company, and who are thoroughly
acquainted with the traditions and manners
of the house.

Such a numerous and homogeneous company in possession of such a vast repertory is
a most singular phenomenon, and one well

worthy of arousing your astonishment. There are, no doubt, in all the great towns of Europe, and especially in London, theatrical companies in which some great actor may be found, like your Henry Irving, some striking individuality perhaps superior to the most eminent actors of the Comédie-Française. But this is an exception, a kind of accidental occurrence. Supposing you brought together for a season two or three great actors, they would no doubt offer very attractive entertainments, but they could not be compared with the Comédie-Française, which possesses a repertory, and which, to use the consecrated expression, *joue d'ensemble*.

So very true is this fact, ladies and gentlemen, that eminent Englishmen have often proposed to copy the organisation of the Comédie-Française, and to establish a similar institution in London, formed on the same model and worked according to the same rules. This idea is no doubt an enticing one: unfortunately it is next to impossible to realise it. If you wish to transplant an old tree, you must, in order to keep it alive, transport along with it the mass of earth in which the roots are embedded: both must be transplanted together and at the same time. In the same way, when it is sought to transport into one country some old institution which has been born and grown, and become great and strong, in some other country, it is necessary to transport along with it the manners and customs from which it derives its life, and all the traditions which create, as it were, a special atmosphere around it, and in the midst of which it can alone be grown. This process is an impracticable one. There is, besides, one element over which we have no command, and that is time.

Certain nations have tried to borrow from you, and to acclimatise in their own country, the parliamentary form of government which it was your glory to be the first to establish in Europe. Nothing was easier than to copy your constitution, to regulate, according to the model furnished by yourselves, the respective rights and duties of the different powers of the State towards one another. But it was not possible to import at the same time the long experience and practice you have had of that constitution, the manners and traditions which form around it a rich soil in which its roots are so firmly and deeply planted — the inviolable respect of the Crown for the rights of Parliament, and the feelings of deference and love for the Crown — the loyalty, in a word — which distinguish the English people. Certain other nations may have assumed all the apparatus, all the outward forms of parliamentary government, but they have lacked the guiding spirit which should animate it, the traditions which support it.

Tradition alone constitutes the power of the Comédie-Française. In order, therefore, thoroughly to understand this ancient institution, it is necessary not so much to study the rules by which it is at present governed, as the whole of the customs and traditions from which it has gradually risen. The cause of its glory can be fully understood only by searching its past history and studying it from its very beginnings.

II

A child, on his birth, brings into the world a certain number of natural dispositions, which, on being developed later by education, will contribute to give the man a character of his own, and tend to form his individuality. Just in the same way there stand, at the origin of all old institutions, one or two initiative facts which gave them a distinctive character, and which regulated their ulterior development. It is necessary to find out and bear these facts in mind, for they are the key to the whole history of an institution.

Two such facts stand at the origin of the Comédie-Française. Both contributed to give it a certain shape and to lead it in a certain direction; the influence of both has acted through centuries, and is still felt to-day.

What are these primordial facts?

Any of you who visited the Paris Exhibition last year may have seen, in the room devoted to the history of the stage, an extremely curious old engraving. It represents a dozen or so actors, wearing their costumes, standing round a table lit up by a candle. He who appears to be the chief is counting out money and dividing it into parts. The engraving is entitled 'After the Performance.'

Such was, in fact, what used to take place. Every night, after the performance, all who belonged to the company, from the manager down to the lowest supernumerary, met together to reckon up the receipts. The total sum was then divided into parts — twelve parts was the number, if I remember right. One actor would receive the whole of a part; another was entitled to half a one; another would get only one-fourth; each according to his importance, merit, and labor, until the whole of the twelve parts were distributed. Thus Molière, the head of the company, received one part in his capacity as manager, and a second one in his capacity as author and actor. It was a kind of coöperative society, which appointed its own manager, and in which every member could be a manager in his turn. This mode of sharing the profits, which certain economists of the present day are trying to adapt to trade and commerce, was put in practice in the first instance by humble actors. It has, with one exception, disappeared from all theaters, where now the director is a kind of foreman or master, and the actors so many paid workmen. It has, however, happily been preserved at the Comédie-Française, which has always been, and is still, a society in which all the shareholders are equal, though possessing different rights.

This is the first of the two primordial facts I alluded to a few minutes ago. The other will not be so easily understood by you, because it is singularly repugnant to English minds. And yet I must ask you to listen to it and to admit it.

In France, under the old régime, nothing could be published without a special authorization of the king. It was a privilege: *cum privilegio regis* are the words which stand on all our old editions. If it were not possible to publish a book without the permission of the king, how much more difficult must it have been to open a theater and act plays without the said permission! The king granted, according to his good pleasure, the privilege to act a certain play in a certain place.

Now privilege means favor, and he who graciously grants the favor is perfectly entitled to exact in return the conditions he pleases. The king who permitted a company to give performances naturally reserved to himself the right to demand that the performances should suit his taste. He would watch over and direct them, and limit them to a certain ideal which he thought to be the best. He was entitled to do this by virtue of the privilege he had granted, and also by virtue of the favors which he was wont to shower on faithful and obedient companies. He sent for them to court, and, on their leaving, loaded them with rich presents. Sometimes he put them down on his private pension list, and paid them a pension every quarter. To-day this would be called a subvention.

Thought, however, even in France, is now emancipated, and the theater is free like the printing-press. But the sovereign — or, if you like it better, the Government — still subventions certain theatrical undertakings, and, like everybody who invests money in a concern, has always the right to examine what use is made of the sum granted. Government, therefore, keeps a right to interfere in these undertakings; and it is thus that the Comédie-Française, which, at its origin, owed its existence to the king, since it received from him first a privilege and then a pension, is still, owing to the subvention it gets from the State, under the hand of the Government.

Here, then, we have two principles before us: the republican principle, since a coöperative society is, according to the formula laid down by one of our most eminent public writers, the government of all by all; and the monarchical principle, since the king in former times and the Government to-day has the right to interfere in the affairs of the society, and to impose his sovereign will on it. One might reasonably imagine that two principles so opposite would either exclude or destroy each other. Well, such is not the case; on the contrary, it is by the action and counter-action of these two principles, always struggling against each other and yet always united, that this great institution, the Comédie-Française, has been formed. We find them at its origin; we can follow their influence as the institution developed itself; to-day they are still contending to get possession of it, and it is that very contest which keeps it alive, for life can be found only where contrary forces struggle and harmonize with one another.

We may discover these same two principles at the origin of all theaters established under the Monarchy. And yet how is it that only one of them, the Comédie-Française, has survived?

It is because that theater had the good fortune to have Molière for its founder and first master. When Molière came to Paris in 1658, a humble author of unknown farces and an obscure comedian, after having completed one of those provincial tours so amusingly described by Scarron in his ' Roman Comique ' there were already two theaters in Paris in a flourishing condition: the Hôtel de Bourgogne, which was the king's theater, and the Théâtre du Marais, where pantomimes were acted. Who would have imagined that the newcomer would so very soon outdo its rivals? The fact is, Molière was not only, next to your Shakspere, or rather by the side of Shakspere, the greatest dramatic writer that ever existed; he was also a clever administrator, an unequalled stage-manager, and an honest man, of large mind and warm heart, adored and respected by his little company, which closely gathered round him like a living organism of which he was the soul.

When he died in 1673, the little company which he had kept united together was on the point of breaking up, and the future Comédie-Française appeared doomed. One of the best actors of Molière, La Thorillière, went over to the enemy's camp — that is to say, joined the Hôtel de Bourgogne. Other defections less important followed. So great an ingratitude towards such a glorious name cannot fail to astonish us. The truth is, Molière was not looked upon by his contemporaries as he is by the present generation. He was not yet transformed into a kind of demi-god. Nobody is a great man during his lifetime, or immediately after his death: time alone completes great men, just as time transforms certain works into masterpieces.

Yes, it is undeniable that time has a great deal to do with the formation of masterpieces. Every generation that passes before a work of genius looks at it from a different point of view, and finds in it new beauties which henceforth remain indelibly attached to it. Time enriches these works with the progress it has made, with the fresh ideas, feelings, and knowledge it has acquired; and it is thus, after the lapse of two long centuries and a half, that we now find concentrated in 'Tartuffe' every kind of social, moral, and religious hypocrisy, as we find every species of jealousy in 'Othello'; it is thus that these characters, enriched daily with the new forms of feeling unceasingly experienced by humanity, assume colossal proportions, and that the poets, who created them, are raised in the eyes of the world to heights of prodigious greatness. Homer perhaps is the greatest poet of all only because he is the oldest, and because three thousand years have labored in his behalf, and made his statue a gigantic one.

We may feel indignant at the thought that the woman to whom Molière bequeathed his name could have changed that glorious name for that of an obscure actor. But we must remember that Molière, in the eyes of his contemporaries, was only a writer of comedies; they did not see in him the great man that centuries have made him for us. His memory was not sufficiently imposing to restrain his old companions from deserting it. There was only one exception, and his humble name deserves to be recorded in history, for it was unquestionably he who saved the Comédie-Française, and, next to Molière, was the real founder of that institution. His name was Lagrange. He was not an actor of great talent, neither had he much intelligence, but he had loved Molière seriously and deeply. If his mind was not large enough to understand the greatness of his genius, he at least felt it in his heart, and he repeated unceasingly to his comrades the words of the humble and the lowly: " Let us love each other in him and through him." The Comédie-Française recently gave this honest man a magnificent proof of its gratitude: it published in a rich form the diary in which Lagrange daily entered the most minute events of the life of Molière's company.

Thanks to him, the company remained united before the public, while the Hôtel de Bourgogne struggled to regain the lead in the theatrical world. The two rival companies fought a hard, and, it must be added, an unsuccessful, campaign. The king resolved to blend them into one. Had he joined Molière's company to that of the Hôtel de Bourgogne, it is probable that the destiny of the Comédie-Française would have taken a different direction. It would have been deprived of that fixed and luminous star, of that lighthouse which has always guided its way through the rocks and

26

shoals of revolution — the name of Molière. But it pleased Louis the Fourteenth, who had always protected Molière and made great use of him, to cast the remnants of the company of the Hôtel de Bourgogne into Molière's company. This fusion took place in 1680. Henceforth there was but one company — the company of the king. The Comédie-Française was definitely established. We, in France, love to call it La Maison de Molière, and that glorious name it fully deserves.

Thanks to the fusion, the repertories of Corneille and Racine were added to that of Molière. It is true that Molière, out of respect for the great Corneille, had played some of his tragedies which the actors of the Hôtel de Bourgogne had rejected. But these tragedies, the works of his old age, were not his best. The great and immortal masterpieces of the poet were the property of the Hôtel de Bourgogne, as was also the repertory of Racine, who, after having been guilty of a petty meanness towards Molière, had quarrelled with him and given his tragedies to the rival actors.

It was a singular fortune, and this happened only once during the lapse of centuries, that three men of genius, very different in character, although nearly equal in talent, should have lived almost at the same time. These three men had written a number of great works, which constituted for the stage a repertory the like of which for richness and beauty has never been excelled. This repertory was an inestimable treasure and an exhaustless resource to the company of the king; for it furnished it with first-rate material to depend upon in times of scarcity; and even now, when we have bad literary seasons to go through, we have recourse to this repertory to satisfy the public curiosity when it is tired and weary of novelties.

III

Such is the starting-point of the organization of the Comédie-Française.

The Comédie is a society, or, should you prefer another expression, a republic, which governs itself. Rome elected two consuls every year; the Comédie-Française elects two chiefs every week, who are styled *semainiers*. Each member is a *semainier* in his turn. The

semainiers on duty draw up the bills of performance, preside over the rehearsals, and
distribute the profits: in short, they are the
captains of the vessel. The engagement of
actors and the reception of pieces take place
at a general meeting of the society.

The king appointed two or four commissioners to preside or to watch over the company; these commissioners, called *les gentilshommes de la chambre,* had for their duty
to enforce the views or taste of the king, and
to defend his interests. And what were their
rights? Exactly the same as those which the
company now exercises, either by itself as a
body, or by the medium of its *semainiers.*
They could make engagements, accept pieces,
impose their programs, and interfere with
everything concerning the theater. Such
were their rights, and they constantly used
them.

But where did the respective limits of
these two rival powers end? As regards
limits, there were none very precise. On one
side, as on the other, there was no law to go
by. If there were written rules, nobody knew
them, or at least paid no attention to them.
Conflicts arose constantly and filled up the

whole of the history of the French stage during the eighteenth century. However, the rival parties generally managed to come to an agreement. How, I can hardly explain, except by comparing the process with the English way of settling difficulties — that is to say, by relying more on common sense and custom than on the technicalities of the law, and by making mutual concessions in accordance with public opinion. For do you imagine that public opinion has had nothing to do with the affairs of the Comédie-Française? No, you cannot think so. The public has been a third power which joined the other two and became the regulator of them. It has played a great part in the history of the Comédie-Française, and it has been one of the most active elements in its final organization. It deserves, therefore, a few words of notice.

Under this name of public or audience, we must not imagine the international crowds which, at the present day, congregate within the theaters of Paris and London. The public to-day is unquestionably a public — there is no other term to describe it — but it is a public devoid of homogeneousness, a compound of individuals who do not know one another, who have no ideas in common, who cannot respond to the same feeling. The public of former days was a real public. On one side were the noblemen who met again at the theater in the evening after having seen each other at court all day long; on the other side were the well-to-do burghers of old Paris, who having closed their shops and done with their business for the day — and at that time, when people did not lead the kind of feverish life we lead nowadays, shops were closed early, and business did not strain the mind — repaired to the play to enjoy their favorite pastime.

The stage in France is a national and especially a Parisian pleasure. Molière, Regnard, Beaumarchais, Voltaire, Scribe, and many other less celebrated dramatic authors were born within sight of the walls of Paris. Everybody in Paris is fond of the play, and is a good judge of it. Even at the present moment, when this passion is not so strong as it used to be, many a young man will go without his dinner in order to treat himself to the play. How many will stand for three or four hours together at the doors of a theater, in the midst of rain or snow, to see the piece in vogue! Everything that relates to dramatic literature is warmly discussed, and there is not a woman, however imperfectly educated she may otherwise be, who is not capable of giving expression to her opinions on theatrical matters, with a knowledge of the subject sometimes astonishing. Every soil has its own peculiar virtues; in the same way every nation has its own peculiar aptitude:

Excudent alii spirantia mollius æra . . .
Tu regere imperio populos, Romane, memento.

The passion of the French is the stage. The Parisian middle class was enraptured with it. Yet, at most, thirty or forty thousand persons went usually to the theater, and out of this number only five or six thousand were regular frequenters. Hence a new piece, after about thirty performances, had exhausted the public interest, and fifteen to twenty performances were considered a fair success. I will not venture to say that all these fanatics of the theater were acquainted one with the other; but they had received the same education, they knew the repertory so well that they could have prompted an actor in distress; they were imbued with the same feelings, and formed those compact and homogeneous audiences, the members of which understood each other perfectly, and by so doing laid down the law of the stage; for, after all, he who pays has a full right to be the master.

The quarrels which divided the actors among themselves, and the actors from the *gentilshommes de la chambre*, were known to these audiences, not by the papers, for there were none, but by the conversations in the *cafés*, and by those numerous imperceptible voices which escape from behind the scenes. They knew that *Messieurs les Gentilshommes* had, in spite of the unwillingness of the committee, engaged such or such an actress, who pleased one of them. The audience, in consequence, revolted unanimously, unless, by chance, the favorite of the court people turned out to be a true artist, and, in this case, they took part against the committee and forced it to give way. However intelligent and discerning it was, the public had none the less its moments of error and passion; in such a case the actors and the *gentils-*

33

hommes united to resist, and, if they held out long enough, they gained the day precisely because reason was on their side.

If you glance over the annals of the Comédie-Française, you will find that the whole of its history is a long series of quarrels and conflicts between the republic of the actors, the personal government of the *gentils-hommes de la chambre,* and that third power, the public, who had no other weapons to fight their battles with but their whistles and hisses.

This public was a jealous and vigilant guardian of tradition. It no doubt accepted the innovations of writers and actors, but it was fond of rules, and reminded the actors of them when they showed signs of departing from them. It was, in fact, the public that made the education of the actors; it placed under their eyes the models of past times, insisting that they be followed; so that in the composition and interpretation of pieces there was no sudden rupture of continuity.

It was thus that the Comédie-Française passed through the brilliant eighteenth century, adding to the repertory of its immortal founders an immense number of works, some

34

of which are veritable masterpieces, while others, less important, form what is called, in theatrical parlance, *le répertoire de second ordre.* Before leaving this subject, let us stop for a moment and consider a circumstance which it is essential to point out, because it has contributed in a great measure to the formation of this repertory, whether of the first or second order.

You have perhaps noticed that, among the great pieces laid before you by the Comédie-Française, several small pieces have slipped in; some are simply vaudevilles and others mere farces. Perhaps you have not well understood how The House of Molière could stoop to such small works. It is because, as I have already pointed out to you, and cannot repeat too often, everything at the Comédie-Française is linked with tradition.

As there was formerly but one theater in Paris which, by virtue of the privilege granted it, alone had the right to give dramatic performances, it was bound to open its doors to pieces of all kinds. In consequence, you will find in the repertory of Molière, by the side of great five-act pieces, *bouffonneries* which in our days would be acted at the Variétés and the Palais-Royal — for instance, the ' Médecin malgré lui ' and the ' Mariage forcé,' not to mention any others. But, as the Comédie-Française assumed more importance in the world of letters, it was obliged to put on a graver tone; it appeared offensive to hear the language of Tabarin on the same stage where, on the previous night, the dignified alexandrines of Corneille had been heard. An incident of Parisian life in the eighteenth century rendered the contrast still more striking.

Every year in Paris two fairs used to be held on public places, which were deserts then, but which are now covered with houses. The more celebrated of the two was the St. Laurent fair, and the older the St. Germain fair. Mountebanks repaired thither in great numbers, and among them were a few stage-managers. These impresarios of the booth came into contact with two privileges: if they desired to make their actors sing, they had the Opéra down on them, for the Opéra alone had the right to charm the ears of the Parisians; if they contented themselves with mere dialogues, they came across the Comédie-Française, which prohibited them, in virtue of its prerogatives, the right of exhibiting speaking characters.

But in France, the classic land of privileges, it must be said that privilege has never been favorably regarded by the public. The people have always taken the side of free competition. Is this feeling one of justice, or is it merely a love of finding fault? I will not attempt to decide. In any case the humble managers of the booth theaters found in the public a benevolent ally as witty as it was noisy. The censorship forbade these strolling companies to indulge in dialogs; so they resorted to mere gestures, while a voice behind the scenes recited the piece as it went on, and the audience applauded enthusiastically. When the moment came for singing a couplet, a great placard was suddenly hoisted in front of the public, on which were written the words and music of the song, and the audience sang the forbidden air, while the actors mimicked the words. The authorities added prohibition to prohibition, but it was all in vain; a thousand ingenious ways of evasion were always found; so they had to retreat, and to allow new theaters to be established with privileges which permitted them to play pieces of an inferior class.

From that moment the Comédie-Française closely confined itself to what are called the serious class of pieces. But, as long as lasted this little war, which amused the eighteenth century so much, and the history of which would take up a whole volume, the Comédie had followed in the track of Molière; it had mixed up farces, comic ballets, and even rhyming burlesques with great works. The tradition was founded; it has been preserved. In addition to certain *bouffonneries* of the classic repertory, the Restoration and the times that followed it up to the present day have taken advantage of this liberty to produce at the House of Molière light pieces like the ' Petit Hôtel ' of Meilhac and Halévy, which was played before you the other day, and gay little comedies, bordering on farce, like the ' Voyage à Dieppe,' in which I have seen Provost and Got many a time.

Another tradition was created by this quarrel between the Comédie-Française and the secondary theaters. It was weak and timid at the beginning, but it has extended considerably of late years, and has become almost a dogma. The time came — (I do not give the precise dates, neither do I enter into details, as it is less a history of the Comédie-Française, than an explanation of the customs and prejudices on which it is founded, that I attempt to give here) — the time came when the pieces of a secondary class, which flourished in the booths of the fair, were received officially on the stage of the Italiens, which had just been dispossessed of its Italian *bouffes*, France having gradually forgotten their language, and fashion having deserted them. A number of ingenious, elegant, and witty authors wrote for this new theater several charming works, which were very successful; among these authors I may especially mention Marivaux and Favart.

The Comédie-Française borrowed from this new repertory some of its prettiest works. For instance, 'Le Jeu de l'Amour et du Hasard,' which had been created at the Italiens by the beautiful and celebrated Sylvia, was transplanted to the House of Molière, to please an actress who was famous at the time, and who thought she would shine in the principal character. The piece, having

39

achieved a success, was placed in the repertory, and is often played at the present time.
It, however, betrays in some ways its origin.
The character of Pasquin requires a deal of
burlesque acting which would appear little
worthy of the Comédie-Française, if we did
not know that it first saw the light on the
boards where the harlequin of the Italians
gave himself up to the coarsest pantaloonery.
They have been kept on the austere stage of
the Comédie-Française, because tradition is
everything there.

During the past fifteen years the Comédie-
Française has practised more extensively than
ever this tradition which Molière has described in the celebrated phrase: " Je reprends
mon bien partout où je le trouve." It is thus
that the ' Gendre de M. Poirier,' the ' Fils
Naturel,' the ' Demi-Monde,' ' Philiberte,'
the ' Marquis de Villemer,' and many more
have been added to the repertory. The
Comédie-Française has become of late a kind
of museum, where good pieces, brought out
at no matter what theater, finally receive
their consecration, in the same way as the
paintings, after having been exhibited during
the life of the painter at the Luxembourg

Museum, pass after his death into the Louvre to take rank among the masterpieces if it be thought they deserve that honor.

While the Comédie-Française was forming for itself an admirable repertory of plays, it was also gathering a marvellous collection of objects of art, statues, busts, and paintings, which might be called its *trésor*, in the same way as we say the *trésor de Notre-Dame*. Who does not know the *foyer* of the Comédie-Française and the gallery which joins it? Who has not admired that superb marble where Molière — an ideal Molière, but no matter — seems to live again, and the pensive face of the aged Corneille, and that masterpiece of masterpieces, the inestimable jewel of the collection, the bust of Rotrou? Shall I speak of the statue of Voltaire sitting, which is known to the whole world by the copies that have been made of it; and of the bust of the same Voltaire which figures by the side of the statue? This Comédie-Française, being a lasting institution, has been able, day by day, and seizing good opportunities, to enrich itself with these marvels of art, of which our Louvre might be jealous. The history of each of these works of art is known, as well as the way the Comédie-Française got them. For this one the artist received a free admittance for life; that one was bequeathed to the house by a lover of the theater; while others were offered by a member of the company, or given by the Government. Every half-century increases the splendor of this collection, and enlarges the library and the archives. The House of Molière is at one and the same time a theater, a palace, and a museum.

IV

All this — repertory, company, collection of art, archives, and glorious mementoes — narrowly escaped destruction or dispersion in the great Revolution of 1789. Politics invaded the house, and divided the members into two hostile camps. The one clung to the old régime and Royalty; the other boldly espoused the new ideas. A schism was inevitable; it broke out. The Royalists remained faithful to the building in which the Comédie-Française was then installed, and which is now the Odéon; the others came and established themselves in the Rue Richelieu, at the same spot where the Théâtre Français is now

to be found. The dissidents were the more
numerous, and, be it said, the most celebrated.
At their head was the illustrious Talma, he
who was to become the glory of tragedy under the First Empire. The public did not
hesitate; they recognized in them the real
heirs of Molière. Moreover, by one of those
dictatorial measures in vogue at the time, the
theater on the left bank of the Seine was
closed, and the actors who had not rallied to
the Republic thrown into prison.

On the 9th of Thermidor there was a moment of inexpressible confusion. All the actors that formed the old company, each going
his own way, were dispersed over various
theaters. But this crisis was a short one; and
in May, 1799, they found themselves united
together again in the *salle* of the Rue Richelieu. All the institutions of the past had
fallen around them; they alone were left
standing uninjured. It was still a republic
governed by consuls elected for a week, and
by their side was the sovereign represented by
a commissioner of the Government. He
loved the theater, did the sovereign, who was
no other than the First Consul. When he
became Emperor, Napoleon the First inter-

ested himself in the house most deeply, and took a proud pleasure in providing a royal audience for his actors in ordinary. He felt the necessity of codifying the customs in virtue of which the Comédie-Française was administered, and he issued the decree which is so celebrated in France under the name of Decree of Moscow. It was indeed from Moscow (1812) that the decree was dated. Napoleon, who had something theatrical and *charlatanesque* about him, did not dislike these contrasts and surprises, with which he thought to dazzle the imagination of posterity. It is useless to enter into the details of this new code; it merely consecrated old usages. The Comédie-Française is still regulated by this code, altho it has been modified by an *ordonnance* delivered in 1830, and by decrees issued in 1850 and 1857. But neither *ordonnances* nor decrees have changed the great features of the company, the only features that interest us in this sketch, and those great features were fixt by Napoleon in accordance with tradition. He added only one point which had its importance as regards the maintenance of the perpetuity of the Comédie-Française through the ages. It had long

44

been the custom that the actors, on retiring after long service, should receive a pension from their colleagues levied on the profits. But it was necessary to provide for the possibility of the company making no profits. Napoleon, besides the annual subvention he allowed to the Comédie-Française, assigned a sum of 200,000 francs as a reserve fund to meet the deficit of bad years and to assure the regular service of the pensions. That measure was not useless, for the House of Molière had hard seasons to pass through.

Of the three elements which have coöperated in the formation and development of the Comédie-Française, we have already seen two at work. And the third? The public — that public of great lords and well-to-do burghers which I described a few minutes ago — that intelligent public, fond of theatrical affairs and jealous of artistic tradition.

The era of *gentilshommes* had passed, and they were no more spoken of. There were still some after the Revolution, but they no longer formed a separate body; they were mixed up with the great public, and, to use the expression of Charles the Tenth, they had, like everybody else, only their places in

45

the pit.   But the middle class public was found again, almost the same as we saw it a few minutes ago: they formed round the orchestra of the Théâtre Français a kind of aristocracy in the matter of taste.   They were called the *habitués* because they went to the theater every night; and when the actor, entering on the stage, perceived those long rows of bald and shining heads, on which the chandelier shed its rays, he was seized with a slight trembling.   I saw the last remnants of this circle in my youth: to-day they have entered into the category of fossils.   It was in talking with them that I learned all that I know about the contemporary theater, for they were nearly all educated persons, men of taste, who went to the play not to be seen, but to see.

But this public of the Restoration and the Monarchy of July committed a grave mistake.   It did not, like its predecessors, hold the balance equal between the respect for tradition and the taste for novelty.   It leaned too much towards the side of tradition, and nearly caused the ruin of the Comédie-Française.   It was natural that the great shock of the Revolution, followed by the magnificent

Imperial epic, should have its influence on literature and the stage — that authors and actors should display to generations, renewed by those prodigious events, new modes of thought and sentiment.

But there is nothing so tenacious as a literary taste. The public of *habitués* had in its childhood admired classic tragedies and comedies in verse, of which the 'Misanthrope' and the 'Femmes Savantes' are the most perfect models. It would not admit of anything outside these two consecrated forms being tried. It might be tired and weary of them, but it would not confess the fact, and gaped and yawned in secret. It rejected with horror every innovation as a scandal; and while in the field of literature that clamorous army known as the Romantic school arose, the Comédie-Française remained obstinately closed to the new art, or, if the latter succeeded in breaking open the door, it was immediately hissed out again, and the *habitués* returned to sleep over the tragedies of the imitators of Campistron, who like himself had imitated Racine.

What was the consequence of all this? The public — I speak of the great public, of that which was composed, as we say in these days, of the *nouvelles couches sociales* — no longer went to the House of Molière. It conceived such a deep hatred of the latest copyists of Corneille, Racine, and Molière, that at length it got disgusted with the masters themselves. The Comédie-Française had hard times to go through then. Receipts of from three hundred to a thousand francs were not rare at that period: the company rubbed its hands with joy when it had (to use the consecrated term) 'passed the four figures,' that is to say, when the receipts amounted to more than a thousand francs. I have in my youth often seen classic works played by a company of eminent actors whose equals we do not possess to-day; altogether there were not more than a dozen of us in the pit, where the price of the places was not more than forty-four sous; the empty boxes looked like so many black holes in the wall; the stalls alone were filled; it was there where the *habitués*, most of whom paid nothing, gathered together.

If the Comédie-Française had not been subventioned, if it had not been under the hand of the Government, it would have broken up at that epoch; for it did not cover its expenses, and each member of the company would have gained more money by playing in another theater. But the members were kept together by the honor of belonging to a national institution, to the *House of Molière,* and by the certainty of a pension regularly paid at the end of their career.

Rachel alone could draw receipts in those times. It was the great Rachel. But Rachel cost the theater more than she ever drew, and she did more harm to art than she rendered it service. She would not become a *sociétaire* or Member, because, once a member, she would have been obliged to share her profits with her fellow-members; she remained a *pensionnaire* (the salaried actors are those who make their first appearance at the Comédie, and are in receipt of salaries until they become Members), because she could demand what salary she liked. The nights on which she played the receipts amounted to ten thousand francs, the whole of which went into her pocket. The next night the theater was empty. Rachel, moreover, must be blamed for having imparted a factitious life to tragedy and for encouraging her admirers to

49

struggle against the advent of a new art. She obstinately confined herself to a dozen parts, in which she displayed incomparable power, and left imperishable memories. She did not lend the assistance of her genius to any of the contemporary poets, or, if she did so, it was with regret, and without decisive success.

V

It was after the Revolution of 1848 that more prosperous, if not more glorious, days began to shine on the Comédie-Française. The commissioners delegated by the Government to this republic of actors had already for some time been replaced by a general administrator. The names had been changed, but in reality the thing was the same. It was still the hand of the sovereign in the affairs of the Company. The rules which limit the action of the two powers are no more defined in the present day than they were two centuries ago. The amount of authority which falls to the general administrator depends on the prestige he enjoys. It is something entirely personal. He is the real master if he is capable and willing. I have known M.

Arsène Houssaye in that post; he was master,
but in such a clever and exquisite manner that
nobody perceived it. M. Empis, on the contrary, acted the master in such a disagreeable
way that he was removed. M. Thierry, who
came next, exercised with all kinds of reti-
cence, circumlocution, and delays, at the same
time appearing to give way, an influence
which was for a long time preponderant.
Finally, M. Perrin, of to-day, has charmed
and overcome all resistance by the clearness
of his views, the brilliancy of his conceptions,
and, above all, by the renown of a successful
and fortunate manager, which he had acquired in all his undertakings, either at the
Opéra or at the Opéra-Comique. And his
good luck has followed him to the Théâtre
Français, for never since its foundation has
the house made such large receipts. They
vary from 6,000 to 7,000 francs. Hence the
dividends shared every year by the *sociétaires*
have become enormous. The Members, besides the salaries they pay to themselves, last
year had parts or shares which amounted to
more than 40,000 francs. Add to this the
supplementary expenses they allow themselves every time they play, or, as ' semain-

ers,' supervise the getting up of a piece; and you will see that a Member entitled to the whole of one part gets from 60,000 to 70,000 francs per annum. Add again the fact that a portion of the profits has been deducted beforehand and turned into two parts, one part to increase the general fund, and the other to form for every Member a little heap of money which he receives on the day of his retirement. It was thus that Bressant, when he took leave of the Comédie-Française, received 80,000 francs in a lump; his retiring pension is, I think, 8,000 to 10,000 francs a year.

It is easy to understand that so many advantages, apart from the honor of being able to put on your card the words, Member of the Comédie-Française, which gives a position in society, and which assures a certain consideration of which actors are all the more jealous that it was long refused to their calling — it is easy to understand that so many advantages possess an irresistible fascination for all young actors. There is not one who does not dream of entering the House of Molière one day, who does not make it the height of his ambition, and struggles with all his might and main to attain it. The high study of elocution would long since have been abandoned for the easier triumphs of the *vaudeville* and the *opérette*, if the House of Molière did not appear in the distance offering its golden apples to candidates. No, you will never know how many unfledged Delaunays and Sarah-Bernhardts there always are on the streets of Paris, who work ten hours a day at the old repertory, and who dine at restaurants at sixpence a head waiting for glory. They try to raise themselves to the height which the Comédie-Française alone maintains in these days of decadence.

The decadence which affects all the theaters in Paris has not yet made itself felt at the Comédie-Française, and yet of the three elements which have contributed to its success during centuries, one has already almost disappeared. There is no longer any public. The Parisian is swamped amid the multitudes which the railways daily turn out on the Boulevards, and which invade the theater of the Rue Richelieu every night. They prolong beyond measure the success of pieces, and force the actors to play them a hundred times running, thereby spoiling talents which

53

cannot be renewed, and which have not opportunities enough to seek fresh strength in the great school of the classic repertory. Their taste is neither delicate nor attentive. They neither instruct nor support the actor. This state of things, unfortunately, will only go on increasing, and I myself can see no remedy for it. It has not yet done much harm to the Comédie-Française, which still presents a majestic aspect, and relies on the two principles which presided over its formation, and which have constituted its power. On the one side, that *ensemble* of actors governing themselves and guarding the traditions. Do you know that between Got and Molière there are only seven or eight names of great actors? We have, so to speak, only to stretch out our hand to be able, across several generations, to find the first Mascarille. Got played a long time with Monrose, who had seen Dazincourt. Dazincourt appeared young by the side of Préville, already old. Préville had known Poisson, who is the last link of the chain up to Molière. In this way the tradition has been preserved alive from one great actor to another. One feels how such or such a part was played in the days

54

of Molière, and when by chance the interpretation is changed by the caprice of an actor, as happened in the case of Arnolphe, whose character was modified by Provost, that change forms a date, and the new tradition is established, unless the successors of Provost reject it. Here we see the distinctive mark of the Comédie-Française, which unites to tradition a wise spirit of innovation, that corrects and harmonises it to the tastes of the day, but at the same time, out of respect for tradition, it always puts the bridle on this taste for novelty. The history of the Comédie-Française is only a perpetual compromise between these two contrary forces.

The administrator represents more especially the spirit of innovation. As he is always a man of influence and education, he brings with him into office personal opinions on art, and seeks to apply them. He therefore gives a stroke to the rudder which turns the ship into a new direction. He is disinterested, as the question of money does not affect him; or rather he has no other interest than glory. He does not, therefore, feel any desire to sacrifice art to big receipts. He is also above those petty rivalries, those mean jealousies, which often divide actors, and from which those of the Comédie-Française are not more exempt than others. He puts an end to their quarrels sometimes by imposing his own will, sometimes by compounding dexterously with their passions. *C'est la lutte: donc c'est la vie.*

Such is it still, this majestic body of traditions, which is called the Comédie-Française. Everything is there, as in great family houses, rich and solemn. The employees of it rest there till old age, and are proud of it. You will find ushers there so ceremonious that they appear as if they dated from the Great Monarch, and had formerly opened the doors to him. The box-openers know all the *habitués*, and salute them with a friendly smile. Costumers and assistants transmit their charges from father to son. The very forms which are used to reply to all who have anything to do with the Comédie smack of old times, and in everything the Comédie says or does there is a politeness and generosity which is like a permanent homage to the memory of Molière.

I think you will forgive a Frenchman for this panegyric. You have enough of other superiorities to admit with a good grace the glory of an institution which is lacking in your country. The people which is to-day at the head of the movement of contemporary philosophy, which has revolutionised the world of thought and science with the writings of such men as Darwin, Herbert Spencer, Sir John Lubbock, and Evans, has nothing to envy in anybody. It is great enough to render justice to the merits of its rivals, and I thank you for having done so with so much courtesy and warmth of heart.

FRANCISQUE SARCEY.

NOTES

As Sarcey has here pointed out the organization of the Comédie-Française is a development from that of the French strolling players of three centuries ago; and it is substantially identical with the primitive organization of the earliest companies of actors in Italy and in England. In those distant days there was no responsible manager engaging all the performers and conducting the enterprise for his own profit and at his own risk. Half a dozen or half a score of the more important actors, after paying salaries to the few who were relatively unimportant, divided the receipts among themselves, share and share alike. They were a self-governing community of equals, altho one of them was necessarily acknowledged as their chief.

As this was the case in France in the time of Molière, so it was in England in the time of Shakspere, who was one of the sharers in the company of which Burbage was the head. The somewhat intricate arrangements between these associated players and the owners of the playhouse are explained clearly in Professor Ashley H. Thorndike's 'Shakspere's Theater' (New York: 1916). And the similar organization of the wandering Italian companies is described in Mr. H. C. Chatfield-Taylor's 'Goldoni' (New York: 1913).

Detailed information about the habits and customs of the French companies, whether they were strolling in the provinces or settled in Paris can be found in 'Le Théâtre Français,' written by Samuel Chappuzeau, published in 1674, and reissued in 1876 with a solidly documented introduction by Georges Monval. As interesting and even more instructive is Eugène Despois' elaborate explanation of the conditions of the theater in France in the reign of Louis XIV (Paris: 1875).

No one of these books is as valuable and as revelatory as is the 'Register' of La Grange in which that loyal follower of Molière set down day by day the titles of the plays performed, the takings at the door of the theater and his own share thereof. Sometimes we can read in this otherwise dry daybook an entry which brings out suddenly the high regard in which Molière was held by his associates. For example, when the company was unexpectedly dispossessed from the theater in the Petit Bourbon and was forced to wait for three months in comparative idleness while the theater in the Palais Royal was being repaired and made ready for them, the rival companies of the Hôtel de Bourgogne and of the theater in the Marais sought in vain to lure away certain of the more attractive actors and actresses; and there is a note of sincere affection in the simple words with which La Grange recorded the fruitless result of these temptations.

The whole company kept together, all the actors loved the Sieur de Molière, their chief, who united to extraordinary merit and capacity an honesty and an engaging manner which compelled them all to protest to him that they wished to share his fortunes and that they would never quit him, whatever proposals might be made to them and whatever advantages they could find elsewhere.

Molière, it must be noted again, was not in any modern sense, the manager of the company; he was only its foremost comedian and its guiding spirit, and he was content to receive only his equal share of the receipts, a share augmented only now and then by small sums specially appropriated by the votes of his appreciative comrades.

In the 'Apology for the Life of Colley Cibber,' we can see how the partnership of a few leading performers in the control of the theater was slowly succeeded by the passing of the management into the hands of one man. And to-day in this twentieth century of ours, the Comédie-Française is almost the only long-enduring institution in which the performers are themselves in power. Yet it is to be recorded that even now there are occasions when a company of actors and actresses, left in the lurch by the failure of their employer, have chosen to fill their engagements as a commonwealth, the minor players taking their humble salaries and the leading players distributing among themselves such moneys as may remain after all the expenses are met.

B. M.

Bei Fragen zur Produktsicherheit wenden Sie sich bitte an:
If you have any questions regarding product safety,
please contact:

Walter de Gruyter GmbH
Genthiner Straße 13
10785 Berlin
productsafety@degruyterbrill.com